THE ON-TIME GOD

by Dr. Ola Adewale

DORRANCE
PUBLISHING CO
EST. 1920
PITTSBURGH, PENNSYLVANIA 15238

Dorrance Publishing Co
585 Alpha Drive
Suite 103
Pittsburgh, PA 15238
Visit our website at *www.dorrancebookstore.com*

ISBN: 979-8-88729-001-0
eISBN: 979-8-88729-501-5

This book is dedicated to God Almighty, the One who is always on time and never late. The One in whom I live, I move, and have my being. To all the people out there waiting on God for one thing or the other, hold on, because there is light at the end of the tunnel!

Contents

ACKNOWLEDGMENTS

I want to thank the Almighty God for the privilege and enablement to write this book. I give Him all the glory for the ideas and wisdom given unto me and the ability to articulate them into words as seen in this book.

My sincere gratitude goes to everyone that has encouraged me, at one time or the other, during the few years it took to finish writing this book - my family, Folakemi Adeosun, Nike Erogbogbo, Bisi Olaoye, Joy Smith, Ladi Babalola and Mrs. Modupe Rowaiye.

To Bisi Olaoye, I say thank you for constantly checking up on me and encouraging me to keep writing. I remember telling you one day that I did not write anything but only proofread what I had written previously. You responded with an encouraging statement saying, "Proofreading is progress, at least you did something." I thank you for the constant nudging.

Tiffany Fuller, thank you for your encouragement and assistance in getting this book published.

I want to say a gigantic thank you to Tola Emmanuel and Afra Bannerman-Fankah, for proofreading this book. Thank you for allowing me to bother you with my numerous texts and thank you for taking time out of your busy schedules to do this. I pray that the Lord will reward you on my behalf and meet your heart desires in Jesus's name.

To everyone that contributed to deciding what the cover page will be, thank you, and to my goddaughters Adeife and Darasimi, yes, it is going to be amazing.

Frequently, we pray and expect that because we prayed, things should happen immediately. When what we have prayed for does not occur, we think God is not listening, or God is not meeting our needs. It is not so. It simply means it is not yet time.

God's timing is different from ours. The Bible tells us that "…A day is like a thousand years to the Lord, and a thousand years is like a day"—2nd Peter 3:8 (NLT).

Also, the book of Ecclesiastes chapter 11, verses 1-11, tells us that there is a time for everything. This means we need to understand the time or season we are in and align with

God's timing so that we are ready to receive the best that God has promised us.

I hope that as we journey through this book, we will position ourselves in God's timetable and enjoy the blessings He has promised us.

As you read this book, I pray it is not just a book but a catalyst for you to believe God for the impossible and trust Him to do it.

Chapter 1

God Cannot Fail

First, I want to say that God is able, and He can. God is God over all the universe, and he is more than able to do what He said He would do. This we see in Numbers 23 verse 19—"God is not a man, so He does not lie. He is not human, so He does not change His mind. Has He ever spoken and failed to act? Has he ever promised and not carried it through?" (NLT)

The above beckons us to God's love and helps us to understand that God cannot fail in whatever He has promised us. It is no wonder the Bible makes us know that "He that hath begun a good work in us will be faithful to complete it" (paraphrased). This statement is the assurance we have that God will never leave us nor forsake us. We are not abandoned projects in His hands because we have the completion of His promise. As we all know, the only one that can start a project and later abandon it, maybe out of frustration, lack of resources, or sheer laziness, is man. God is never frustrated or lazy, and He can never lack the resources needed to complete the good work He has started in our lives.

When God said, "…I will never fail. I will never abandon you" (Hebrews 13:5, NLT), He meant it. He does not play with words as we humans do. Due to situations we find ourselves in, circumstances we face, or challenges we find ourselves in daily, we often think that God has left us, but no! He is always with us every step of the way. We are encouraged in the Bible to give thanks in every situation or circumstance we find ourselves in, and that "all" things work together for our good. The emphasis is on the word "all." Whether good or bad, "all" will work for our good because God is in control.

What does it mean to fail?
According to Merriam-Webster's dictionary, some definition of the word fail is to lose strength, to fade or die away, to stop functioning normally, to become absent or inadequate, to be unsuccessful, and to neglect or abandon. The common factor in all of these definitions is that none describes the character of God. God cannot lose strength, cannot fade or die, cannot stop functioning normally, is never absent or inadequate, can never be unsuccessful, and can never abandon us because He has promised not to leave us nor forsake us (Hebrews 13:5, KJV).

God's thoughts towards us are good and not evil, with the promise to bring us to an expected end. If He has promised us and He is not a man that lies, He is obligated to bring to fulfillment all that He has promised. Knowing fully well that He cannot fail, we should be rest assured that whatever He has said concerning us will surely come to pass. God will not fail us in the establishment of His promises because His name is at stake.

So, we need to remember always that GOD CANNOT FAIL. He that hath begun a good work in us will be faithful to complete it until the coming of the Lord Jesus Christ (Philippians 1:6, KJV, paraphrased).

CHAPTER 2

FROM BELIEVE TO TRUST

Why do we need to believe or trust God?

To believe means to accept as true, to trust in, or to hold as an opinion. To trust on the other hand means reliance on another, assured hope, depend or have faith in. Based on these definitions, I am sure you will agree with this next statement—to trust is a higher level of believing. For us to align with the plan of God for our lives, we need to move from the place of believing God to the place of trusting Him. When we get to the latter, we are saying we rely on Him, we depend on Him, and we trust that there is nothing He cannot do, as seen in Luke 1:37 "with God nothing shall be impossible." We must trust that God will do it in His own time.

As a child, I had so much faith and trust in my parents especially when it pertained to things I wanted. I did not care to think if they could afford it or not; I just had so much reliance on them that anything I wanted will surely be provided for me. This is exactly how God asks that we come to Him, like little children. The Amplified version of the Bible rightly describes it in Luke 18:17—"I assure you, whoever does not receive the kingdom of God [with faith and humility] like a child will not enter it at all." We, as children of God, should come to God with the kind of trust a child has in their father and mother that they can provide what the child wants.

Have you ever been privileged to listen to children boasting about their parents? Especially their fathers? Children boast and expect that when their father shows up on the scene and is put to test, he will not fail. They have so much faith and trust in their father not to disappoint them. This is the same way God wants us to boast about Him, and trust him to show up and show off concerning that which we have boasted of. In Proverbs 3:5–6 we are enjoined to: "Trust in the Lord with all your heart; do not depend on your own understanding. Seek His will in all you do, and He will show you which path to take" (NLT). Trusting God with all our heart means to abandon ourselves in God, totally and completely rely on Him, and depend on him without wavering. When we do all these and acknowledge Him in all our ways then He will show us the path to take—the path that leads to the best place because He is the one leading. When God leads and we follow, the combination puts us on the path of God's plan and purpose for our lives and ultimately aligns us with His timetable and timeline for us.

For instance, children often play "catch" with their parents, which is when they pretend to fall or even jump into the arms of their parents from an elevated place. They do so without thinking for a moment whether the parent will catch them or not (this is trust). The main reason the child would jump without fear is because of the trust he/she has in the parent giving that confidence that they will be caught before hitting the floor. This is the kind of child-like faith God wants us to come to Him with, trusting Him without a doubt.

We as individuals need to come to the same point as the three Hebrew boys, Shadrach, Meshach, and Abednego in Daniel chapter three. They refused to bow to the golden statue made by the King of Babylon even when threatened with the fiery burning furnace. They believed God was able to deliver them and chose not to bow even if God did not deliver them. Why were they able to make this boast? The answer is "trust." The trust they had in God that He was not going to abandon them in the furnace and would show up for them. They took to heart the scripture that God has called us His faithful to preserve that which is committed into His hands (paraphrased). They trusted God with their lives, truly believed that He will not leave them nor forsake them, and God showed up for them. In the layman's language, he showed up big time as seen in verse twenty-five of chapter three of the book of Daniel. He is described as the fourth man in the fire whose form is like the Son of God. Their trust in the Almighty God delivered them and He can do the same for us as we learn to **TRUST** Him.

Trust him to show up for us when we need Him the most. Trust him never to leave us nor forsake us. Trust Him to preserve our lives, trust him to catch us when we are falling, and trust Him to lead us on the right path.

Chapter 3

Mean Time and Set Time

Oftentimes our perseverance and patience are put to test by the situations or circumstances we find ourselves in. What we do during the time of testing makes a whole lot of difference as it determines the outcome of the situation or circumstance. As we go through this chapter, I want us to keep in mind that the quality of the harvest influences how long you have to wait for the fruit. For example, corn is harvested in three months, yam in about six months, and cocoa in about three years. Guess what? Corn is the cheapest, and cocoa is the most expensive of all three.

Having said this, let us drive the point home by relating it to when we pray and are believing God for something(s). The time of waiting for an answer after praying is the time our perseverance and patience are put to test. The time between the last "amen" to our prayers and the manifestation of that which we prayed for is known as the "meantime," while the time when we have what we prayed for is the "set-time."

Meantime

The Merriam-Webster dictionary defines the meantime as "the time before something happens or before a specified period ends." However, for us, the meantime is the time between saying amen to our prayers and receiving the answers to our prayers (the set time). What we do in the meantime plays an enormous role in the outcome of the prayer we have prayed. The meantime is a time of trials, temptations, perseverance, endurance, and patience. The meantime is not the time to complain but a time to praise God (though hard to do) better than we have ever done, and a time to appreciate Him more with the mindset that we may never have the opportunity to do so again. The meantime is the time to confess positively despite the several opportunities that come our way which may want us to confess otherwise. We have to consciously (note I said consciously) make every effort not to be negative but positive in all we say, do, or think.

Set Time

The set time is the time when all things fall into place, our prayers come to fruition, and there is a physical manifestation of that which we prayed about. The set time is "now"—this moment. The Bible describes it in Psalm 102 verse 13 saying, "Thou shalt arise and have mercy upon Zion: for the time to favor her, yea, the set time, is come." The set time is not known by anyone, except God Himself. The realization of the set time, from the moment we say amen to our prayers, may be short or long. An important thing to do is to prepare for the set time so that we are ready when it comes along. Examples of getting ready for the set time may include something as big as buying a car seat and crib if believing God for a child or as little as buying a keychain if believing God for a car.

During the meantime, getting ready and preparing for the realization of the answers to our prayers helps us to ease into God's blessings easily when the set time arrives.

Both the meantime and set time have the same bedrock called "faith." We must remember that the Lord is the faithful One that has promised to hear us and to make impossibilities possible when we believe. Luke chapter 1, verse 37 (paraphrased), says that when we believe, there shall be a performance (coming to pass) of the things spoken to us by God.

I pray that as you read this book with me, the set time for us will come sooner than we can imagine. Be expectant, hold on because the set time is here and we must continue to take steps that will get us closer to our set time.

Chapter 4

What is Your Time?

Yes, what is your time, and no, I am not referring to the time on the clock.

What time are you in now? Are you in the time of waiting? Time of believing? The time of trusting? The time of hoping? Or even the "about to give up" time? It does not matter what time you are in; all that matters is God's time. The key to pulling through in whatever time we find ourselves in, is to align with God's time. There is a popular phrase that we have all heard at some point—"God's time is the best time." It is the best because God can never get it wrong.

God's timing is different from our timing. When we think all is lost, God says, "It is found." When a man says it is over, God says, "I am just starting". When we think, "How am I going to get out of this mess?" God says, "My grace is sufficient for you."

The book of Ecclesiastes chapter three, verse two says, "A time to be born and a time to die; a time to plant, and a time to pluck up that which is planted." It emphasizes the notion that there is a time for everything. If we plant and try to harvest before harvest time, we will probably get unripe fruit or a bad seed. It is easier said than done, but it is not impossible to align our time with God's time.

How do we then align with God's timing?
The first step to aligning with God's timing is learning to listen to God when we pray. We align with His timing by calling those things that are not as though they were. We do this by shifting our focus from asking Him to

thanking Him. We do this by praising God for those things we already have and much more for those things we do not have yet. Thanking God for those things we do not yet have is very important because it means that we trust Him to do them and we technically "put God on the spot." He is a good and faithful God, who shows up big time whenever we "put Him on the spot" by boasting about Him. It is almost like His name is at stake, so He shows up.

Aligning with God's time means handing over everything to Him. It is getting to the level of the three Hebrew boys—Shadrach, Meshach, and Abednego—when they refused to bow to Nebuchadnezzar's statue and said they were certain God would deliver them from the fiery furnace. The three of them went further to say that even if God did not deliver them, they were ready to perish than deny their God. Guess what they were doing? They were boasting about God, and He showed up big time as the fourth man in the fire.

Aligning with God's time is saying, "Father, let your will be done in my life." After this has been said, the next step is to lay it at His feet, which means not having a plan B, but trusting God to do what we have asked of Him.

In this process of aligning with God's time, the idea is not to claim the waiting game without doing what needs to be done. What do I mean by this? It means, for instance, improving ourselves if we need to. Do you need to take that course? Then do it. Do you need to relocate? After prayerfully asking God and receiving the go-ahead, then do it. Do you need to make a phone call? Then do it. The list goes on and on but I guess you got the gist.

Therefore, whatever time we are currently in, let it line up with God's time and watch Him show up as He always does.

CHAPTER 5

THE ON-TIME GOD

Yes, that is who our God is—the on-time God. He is never late. Although it may seem like the manifestation of the prayer request is taking forever, He always shows up at the right time.

Let me explain this in layman's terms as we say. Let's depict two characters in a movie, the good guy and the bad guy. We reach moments where it seems the bad guy has the upper hand, but suddenly, the good guy gains a dominant position, and the story takes a new turn. This is precisely what happens when we are trusting God for something. In our little minds, we think because God did not show up with our answer the moment we prayed, we feel rejected. We start to count the days, weeks, months, and sometimes years, and in one moment and in a twinkle of an eye, the One who is never late, the one who is outside time and space, the one who is God in the company of gods, the Almighty God, shows up on the scene, and the rest is history.

Remember, God will always show up when it is the "set time," and nothing or no one can stop that time from being; we just need to wait for it. You may have heard of the phrase "No condition is permanent." This is true—no condition lasts forever, and regardless of what we may be going through, we need to know that it is not permanent. There is a set time for it to be over.

For instance, when God asked Abraham to sacrifice his son, Isaac, he obeyed and tied up Isaac to be sacrificed, but before he could slaughter his only son, the "On-Time God" showed up in His glory and provided a sacrificial lamb. Another story that readily comes to mind is Jesus raising Lazarus from the dead. Everyone had given up hope including his sisters but guess what? The "On-Time God" showed up! He showed up, not a day before, but on the third day which was the set time for that miracle. There are many more instances of God showing up for people when all hope was lost as we explore the Bible. The same God that did it several thousand years ago remains the same today.

The attribute of God as the "On-Time God" can be encapsulated in two scriptures. Firstly, Mark 11:24 says, "Therefore I say unto you, what things soever ye desire, when ye pray, believe that ye receive them, and ye shall have them" (KJV). This scripture says when we pray, all we need to do is believe and we are guaranteed to receive that which we prayed for. Secondly, Ephesians 3:20 says,

"Now unto Him, that is able to do exceeding abundantly above all that we ask or think, according to the power that worketh in us" (KJV). God is able to do it, period! The question is when? This we were not told but what we do know from the scripture is that he is able to do. The scripture goes on to say according to the power that works in us. What is this power? Our faith in God, our belief in Him, and most importantly, our trust in Him to do what He said He will do.

CHAPTER 6

KEYING IN

What is the conclusion thereof? Listed below are a few take-homes for us from this journey.

Firstly, there is always a light at the end of the tunnel, and we need to keep driving to get to the light. We should not dwell on the happenings but be focused on the outcome of our passing through. Always remember the promise of God to us in Jeremiah 29, verse 11, which says, "For I know the thoughts that I think toward you, saith the Lord, thoughts of peace, and not of evil, to give you an expected end" (KJV). The expected end referred to here is a good one considering His thoughts towards us are good. Therefore, as you go through the tunnel, focus on the expected end which varies for each individual. My expected end may be a new home while someone else's may be a child or a job. The bottom line is to be focused on your expected end.

Secondly, God has numerous ways through which He can meet our needs, and sometimes, we may be looking in the direction He is not coming from. God may not be in the wind, in the earthquake, in the fire, but He may be in the still small voice (1st Kings 19, verses 11–12, KJV).

Thirdly, remember that sometimes the start of a thing may not be as easy as we would like it to be, but if we stay on track and continue the process, our result could be better. Job chapter eight, verse seven, says, "Though thy beginning was small, yet thy latter end should greatly increase." This is a promise from God reminding us that we should not be discouraged when the process seems not to be working or seems to be taking longer than expected.

Finally, as we continue on this journey, let us remember that there is a set time and the meantime. What we do in the meantime affects the happenings in our set time, and God is always on time.

REFERENCES

1. All Scriptural references unless otherwise specified are taken from Holy Bible, King James Version, and is in the Public Domain use from www.biblegateway.com

2. Scripture quotations marked NLT are taken from the Holy Bible, New Living Translation, copyright © 1996, 2004, 2015 by Tyndale House Foundation. Used by permission of Tyndale House Publishers, Inc., Carol Stream, Illinois 60188. All rights reserved. www.biblegateway.com